To Kill a Poet

A Collection of Poems

notionpress.com

To Kill a Poet

A Collection Of Poems

Shanta Jayaram

notionpress.com

Notion Press

Old No. 38, New No. 6

McNichols Road, Chetpet

Chennai - 600 031

First Published by Notion Press 2016

ISBN 978-93-86009-06-7

Contents

Preface

Standing near the kitchen back-door with my mother, pointing to a large Colocasia leaf with a big dew drop shining in its middle, I asked her, "What's that?"

"It's the baby of the leaf" she replied, not taking her eyes off the leaf, I too stared at it. It was early in the morning. I was maybe a two or three years old.

Our home was in the then fledging township of Rourkela. A steel township in the eastern part of India, Odisha State, known as Orissa, back then.

The howls of jackals, I still recall. As night fell we would huddle into our tents. That was our home till houses were built and the Steel Plant township grew.

My father a metallurgist, pioneered along with a few others in creating the township and the Steel Plant.

The grounds we walked on then, were wild with short shrubs on flat, hard, yellow soil. The shrubs, a little shorter than me had small, oily pods, pointed leaves and tiny white flowers.

Once as we walked through the oily pods and pointed leaves, I asked the woman, accompanying me, "Why are we here?"

"*Hava khane*" (To eat air) she replied in Hindi.

"*kaise*?" (How) curious, I asked.

"*Muh khol ke rakkho*", (Keep your mouth open) or some words to this effect, she answered.

I did what she said, kept my mouth open to eat air, for quite some time. It was not comfortable.

I remember the walk, also the trip down the fresh dug ditch of red mud that I could not cross and the laughs that followed. And my laughs too.

Some good laughs. Some not so good.

Yet, all inspirational!

With heartfelt gratitude and sincerity I acknowledge all who have made this volume possible.

The three Su's of my life, their wonderful life partners. My mother and father for letting me, be. My brother, whom I loved dearly, my sister, who is far away. My dearest friends from school and college, I acknowledge too.

And, the One who stood by me.

Thank you Notion Press, it's a lease of life for writers like me. Thank you, Naveen and your team, for your constant support.

Gracy, Janardhan, Neil and Ann, a big thank you.

100 Meters or So

100 meters or so
On jelly path flat,
A tireless, elliptical walk mine.
Face East, face gate of two-leaves.
Turn West, climb wall on wall.
East, Deep trees, huge sun rays tilt.
West, embers drunken, fling
Gulmuhur, Copper pods.

Milk-tree jasmine,
Trimmed umbrella each,
Pure white flowers stars!
Supple lives many,
Shelter stories many,
A boundary liquid with so many!
A mundane growth for many.
Periphery
My walk.

Much, much, suckled I
At milk-tree jasmine,
And played Mynah
In and out,
In and out.

To worm search
To Sustenance clutch
In dust scratched
In must cavorted
Confabulations had,
With sky showers
With sharp thrust of drops,
We, in hollows hid.
The Boundaries held,
My elliptical walk
On jelly path flat,
100 metres or so

Open
House door.
Why enter?
Woman!

Glint, Gold fish!
Silence, lively waters.
Aquiline Grass, ride
Caterpillar arched bead back.
Trapeze Bulbul artist
On stalk slender dangle.
Boat away! Crane
Cover monsoon sky pink.
Or zig-zag off,
Drachm Dragonfly!

Burst brain!
To Exaggeration!
To Countless
Million Thoughts
In Abstraction live!
On jelly path flat
100 meters or so.

Again

Newspaper
Tea-sips
Body your
Covers

Again!
Mynah's Eyes with
I see
Palm frond, drape
Palm trunk.
Leave top freshness,
Summer's fruit,
Little by little,
At dawn on dawn.
To meet,
Mud wetness.
Grass shoots.
First time!

Butterfly Proboscis with
I taste
Sunlit light,
Ether drops,
Lustrous dews,
On Tulsi twigs.

Little by little,
At dawn on dawn.
To meet,
Scented Mud,
Silver snails,
First time!

Lotus Pores with
I smell
Water's cool,
Lichen shades beneath.
Ariel roots,
Ancient Banyan throws,
Martian berries drop.
Little by little
At dawn on dawn
To meet,
Firm mud.
Fish waters.
First time!

Breeze Arms with
I hold
Humming wings,
On full tree tops.
Brush blooms!
Flowers pink pelt.
Little by little

At dawn on dawn
To reach
Her palms,
Win hearts,
Always!

Ochre Veins with
I hear
Direct blaze,
On dark rocks,
Cup small waters,
With crackling Sunbits.
Little by little
At dawn on dawn
To reach
Inside all
Anad Aum
Somehow!

Again
And
Again!

To Kill a Poet

When you turn,
Flame moth
To a monkey!
Its wings spread wide,
Hazy gauze!
To a Tail, hairy.
Its Passion, love-crazed,
To an antic, curled in nit picking

And turn,
Oil-lamp,
To a fixed Electric bulb.
Its shadow reflections and
Glow spreadnessness,
To a Switch-click.
Its Pictures, seamless
Aligned to One choice
On or Off?

And Turn,
Always fresh Nude Body,
To a Parcel.
Its Cells, alive of hundred twenty five years
To a sticky cell-o-tape.

Its Sensory Organs growing many secrets,
To Text book easy, in paper tear-aways,
Stapled and book bound.

And Turn
Tree Juhi subtle scented spilling euphoria
From countless minute flowers,
To a mesh of wires, scissored.
Its Blanket forgivenessness
To a Cup-of-Bonsai, pruned.
Its proclaimed resurgence,
To a spot-of-corner, rusty hook.

And Turn
Sleeping Crows on Gulmuhur branches
To shod foot junta about, trundling.
Their startle sharp at slightest stir, all winging!
To heads bent low, shoes stalking.
All Crows night long search,
To shod foot in mustard splutters picking,
Glee at many doors.

And Turn
Unapologetic Beauty
To Nadir's stare.
In tenacious truth, its roots,
Skinned pink by force
It's fibres raw relegated,
To dead pool of Narcissist.

And Turn
Piquancy of Night to
Day half long.

Its Intoxicants,
Hung in forgotten halls,
In Sepia mounted pictures.

Its Brimmings,
In forgotten garden, some
In a Names list, over stone plaque.

It's Music
Piteous! Keyed in from jukebox there kept.
In repetitive dirge, somber.

Virtually so
Into Sun's Fire then
Luminescence of Night
Burn

For
To Create
Not
Is
It's Indigo!

To Fallow
Is
It's Seeds!

To Abstinence
Is
It's Givings!

To Stoicism
Is
It's Pledges.

Quickly,
So quickly
Then
You will
A Poet kill
A Universe annihilate

Aggression!

AM 7
Bang, Bang!
Hammer hard! Hammer rough!
Broken bricks, slit tiles,
Rotten beams, sticky
Termites, bent nails,
Falling
Crash!
Red-oxide Floor
Cracks!

Scrape hard, scrape rough!
Old peels fast fall,
Off humungous doors windows.
Shavings of wood,
Musty sharp
Faint of paint,
Stirred by his gnarled feet,
Muddy my very old home of lime wall

AM 10
Water! Food!
All!
Money! Clothes!
I Must! I Must!

Screams She!
Screeches She!
Broomstick curls
Dry stick out
Holler from flat occiput.

Beats her breasts.
Belly of 28 years,
Wrinkled pits,
Life shows.
Odoriferous!
Perspiration pours.
Sours of maids!
Cheapens me to my face,
To the twitters of
The bashful Bakul tree

PM 1.30
"Eat fast!
Ooopen quickly!
Cls ur mouth!"
Feeder raves.
Every day.
Twice a day.
Wails two year old
At aberration of mother
Chokes!

"To Balcony, out!"
Out.
She locks him out.
He peers inside,
Knocks his head
On glass door shut.
In Hot sun
Waits...
Damned Both.
Pistol damnation
To me
Through fengshuied balcony

PM 4
"Caesar up!
Caesaaaa run!"
Commands Racqueter.
Racquet flailing,
Flailing to strike.
Careens limpid lab,
11 years sad,
Into Caesar 2,
Shepherd bad.

In limpid son's,
Plaintive grapple.
Lunges shepherd
Fangs glare.

Lab yelps at dark bites
Lab howls at fixtures all.
Docks me
In mortified piss,
Wide cattle-trap within

PM 10 & beyond
Steel spoons, Food plates clatter
The Dinner time's on.
Every night, everyday
Television swarms,
Forks out my India's lot.

To His and Hers
My Earth cut!
Oh Saints!
Will She
Of Knowledge
Ever shy!
Ever sit
Her Peacock Throne
On Shame?

Bead soon
Oh Feeler!
A new Suprabhat song

While night
Covers all.

To sign
Indictment of souls
How?
Mine Weeps
To blotches of ink...

A Shadow

A Shadow
Path crosses ours, so wistfully carved...
Our cherished path!
And Rudes it,
To rubble

Cat and Crow,
Appear,
Black.
A Bane
Or Boon
Or a Belief
That proves.
Anyone?
They Appear,
Wait and Tell,
A shadow
Tails our purple wish

To Asunder
A Shadow
How?

And
Trace Quick
The Moment

So pristine
Dew like
A jewel
Ensconced in
Beyond

Then quick
Close eyes
Clasp palm
Trap wish!
Wish!

Live true!
Then on
Perchance
The Purple Wish,
Might Just come by...

While a Shadow Tails...

Will Some Body With Me Not Dally?

Will Some Body
With me not dally?
Fill love chasms in
Monument of Body
For shine,
Place Jasmines,
So many!
To senses divine
Then esteem
Our Blossoms,
Them, beg
Not to die!

Bursts!
Bougainvillea flame crest
Crests chill night's wants
At what heights!
Tight ambers,
Wish awakens!
Jewels ophidian's glance

Watch!
Dark Neem nimble
Cool Chandrima's blue fire

Burn white flowerings
From seared iron bowers

Flout!
Rectitude of night velvet
Its swathes rustle to dance
In upswing throw fretting bird
In high to cry
In moist glisten lost

Do Some Body with me
To nectar sip,
Slip away, to
Cup seven skies
From painted flowers wild
In waters torn,
On weathered slopes grown

Live!
Art
Of Splendours
Senses to
Sensuous
Bow

Till sparkles reach
Cold flesh pores.
Full in freshness then,
As Body honeyed brims

Quiet lie
O! Absorber
Revel!
As Bee
Reaches out from
Hive honey rich.

Body Feels Gold

Body feels Gold
Sunshine I rubbed
Lain on cement slab
Now reposeful
Magenta begins!
Evening-blossoms corner
Earth pulls!
Milk-tree jasmine
Shoe flower pistil
Inter-space pulsates!
Will secrets reveal?

Body feels Silver
Moon-kohl I smeared
Still on cement slab
More acute
Covert Chandan in young
Guava branches course,
Hide Original flower filigree

Lone Serenader,
Lit up
Wings hurry
On Filigiree lights

Flurries! Hurries!
Earnest Circumambulates
Holds out, Why?

Rains, don't!
Just
So I blink
Lashes
Eyes close
And
You
Slip away...
Before Body blurs!

Butterfly Rare

And fly! Butterfly rare
Why? Touch me you did!
Over swarming floods aced,
Leaving cussed skies dismal
And raw beautified

My Georgette white,
Large sky-flowers imprinted with
You caught?

Or, My Smell white,
Flood thoughts oozing
Limbs yours swayed?

Or, My aghast Core white
Flood waters petrified,
To you limped?

Whichever you say
Why! Touch me you did!
And raw beautified
Bye, Butterfly rare
Over flood waters fly!

And Water born again, I
Will test,
Loved so
As loved once before,
White waters again
A Butterfly rare.

Battered Gate

Battered gate stood still while
The important materials carrier,
The truck with trailer,
Revved Hurtling,
Again and again hit.
Gate creaked on hinges,
Impaled to ground.
For welcome, opened.
For safety, closed.
Till water, concrete 'n jelly,
For it two pillars built.
To hold light domes,
That showed the ways
Of the hurtling, revving truck,
Losing control,
Hushed! In a ditch
Condemned scrape was
Anyways.

Story ends.

Buffalo Stroll

Have you seen Boy Buffalo stroll?
Unexpected come
From behind
Illegal houses matchless!
Thematic India floor.
But how can
He, encroachments know?
Thatched roof 'n four poles under,
Open drain filled
Rainwater with not
But Ugh
He resides besides one of them,
In the fuming Banners filled road.

Away, once, early
On awry mud path
Stealing breaths of air of...
Whatever you dare say!
Quickens his pace,
Marvels at
Marvels, dunked in ash.

Unmoving donkeys five,
Hooves in loops tied.
Conical long baskets two
Flung to their sides.

To carry more bricks
For more structures to raise
Atypical, all.
Such ground breaking rights!
Just plumb for any site.

Boy buffalo strolls
Bits of grass tastes,
Off toothless gums spits
Rain fed grass red!
To eat
Not fit!
"Sorry, the brunch failed
Man for his dirty bricks, be jailed"
His head he shakes.
The Donkeys down cast their eyes.

A bass bellow he hears!
Dhaivata! He knows she is near
As always a U-turn he takes
And tries to meet her gait
Boy 'n girl together
Search watering hole to
Go 'n go 'n go to places
Want to know some more?
Elephants, horses, Camels, then
Strike off from your rolls.
And take a boy buffalo stroll.

Buffalo Eat

Have you seen Buffalo eat?
Off offal rubbish
In garbaged street.
Search for paper bits,
Some vegetable peels
In stink-in-vogue,
Bacteria
Birthing
Peat!
Poor! Big girl
In high-tech terminal city
Parked in filth 'n more
In never-die plastics!

Beside her squats
A sweat stained slur.
At her teat tugs,
Calloused hands with
Oil smeared wraps,
Angles the squirts, flow just
Quickly for milk to pour.
It did not supply?
Question does not apply.

Reed knotty lands
Whack! Whack! Whack!
On back, on flanks, on back,
Fright Startles, flow just!

Perchance the mute
Otherwise decides,
A still lying calf,
Propped is, to the side,
Happy squirts the flow just
To hit pale waters,
Steel pail inside.
A modicum of modernity,
With best food yet!

Railing at the sight!
The plight of
Buffalo eat
In stink-in-vogue
Bacterial peat
Recommends the Feeler
To Bloomers 'n Lippers
Of cattle menace yet.

Parked in sanctified
Offices with pictures
Of gods, flowers 'n all.

Masters of stories,
Seated in harmony
Warming 'n downing
Milk 'n tea 'n coffee
Cups 'n cups yet
You!
Plastic peats
The best!
Ahoy!

Buffalo Jump!

Have you seen
Fat buffalo jump?
Funny to see
Fat Buffalo jump

Down up down
Excitement of
Big, Half-a-ton.
In suit black, proper.
Kick back thick hooves,
Exhale air gust
Nostrils soft moisten.
Bellow and ready,
Momentum runs!
On slippery trail,
Oh! Toast of greens
Crack tiny snails
Tranquillity jumps!

Squelch and pulp
Greens in wade.
Paddle to a vintage
Hiding lots of rain!

Down up down
Jump Jump Jump!
Neck, swing-a bit
Ears hot, flip, flip, flip
It was a lumbering run!

Green cud chews,
Jaws little move.
Down in rain sinks,
Up, heaves again.

Mud-packed back,
Green-caked horns,
Long grass streamers,
Over bulb eyes.

Swish tail swish,
On Incorrigible flies land
Oh! But the smell sweet,
Of Buffalo-land!
The pests land back.
Firm in ownership of
Large leather-land.

Leap-frog brethren
Smote to the core
Red at prickly blow
Leap for bulrush ready,
Indecision palpitates, to
Top go or look below

Happy fellow buffalo
Nonchalant bellows happy!
Happy the fellow in greens,
To day 'n night long play
Down up down
And in rains Jump!

Wish I, a 'Guy' or
Buffalo
In greens to stand,
Day n' Night long
Play
Whistle
Bellow
And, In rains
Jump!

Child I

Child I
Breeze tail hold
Cloud float
In skies

Old age aches.
Hollow bones.
Hide thief,
Hide!

Sunshine mirths,
On Tall grass rolls.
On pushes Breeze,
Rolling Tall grass
Round 'n round
Round 'n round

Away from the Sun!
It's different fun.
Sunshine prowls,
The truant one,
In heady grass smell
Marks a pit,
To hide away a bit.

And as tall grass caves,
And large circles made,
In a perfect one
Large Pollen warm
In repose curls...

But always
Sunshine as opines
Chases 'n grips
Could be Squirrel or fish
Down clamp long paws
Hot? Just squirm a bit
Let go!

Clap and Slap

Claps wide in distance, thunder
Quickly music shall downpour
Aha to you,
Drummer of sky
Razzle-Dazzle
In crisscross lightning
A nuanced beat.
Trail of treat.
A strong bass,
Long low.
A silence sudden,
Excitement curling,
A rhythmic blast!
Deafening mutiny.
Early morning,
Pure amplified,
Over quietness,
In deepening, crumpling, cloudy skies

Retail Outlet while
Clanking uprolls,
Iron shutters serrated all,
In fatness chain
Lengths of metal
Laboriously coiled
Circular wheels over.

Near Ear,
Grinding, Intolerable
Gratings slap!

Music of Dawn.
Sullied!
Un-dignified

For compose
To silent Palm trove
Thoughts run, mine wildered!
Close hug Thorn palm, worn
The shame for
To hide.

Sisters

Like raga we curled
In mother's womb
In waters primordial, grew
Conch pitch, did they
To Primordial Naad?
Just when we cried?
For brothers they do
Our very own,
Toss joy, lime yellow in air!
For us, it's kept at altars ware
With Chosen songs to sing.
Cat gave us a Ladle, a spoon,
A Quirk, visage dark or fair.
The Hidden Creator,
There is. True, they say.
Why then!
Our wombs no ware!
O! Tulasi
Yet, Sisters we cannot be.

Down ages in braids
We played and chased
Caches of tree stock gusty fall
In blazing sun and burning, whirling
Winds, wild twirlings scooped,
Jokers jumping as hot mud they hit!

Gave names and cried
"Mahua!" "Jamune!" "Gulmuhur!" "Bakul!"
Hot, blue, red, scented all!
My raiment cradle you filled with pick
For yourself, shied away from all
Doled you I, a this and that
Stale ones sometimes,
Many times at that.
You nodded and took
You did. Why?
Did I tell you to?
Ah! Tulasi!
Yet Sisters we cannot be.

Raced I into forest streams, hiding
Away from kutir's
Sanctimonious walls.
Breathless you cried
"Trust not treacherous waters,
They play to play n hide"
Into them yet I dived for frolic
A hedonist for a prince's loving splurge
But! The waters cruel destroyed it all
Our band of love, his ring I lost.
It just slipped off my finger creamy soft
The curse had worked
"You, Who?" He deigned to ask.
Slashed I in forest. Barbs boomed. "You, who?"
You wept in shame and pain for me

Feared punishings of sanctimonious pride
You dived the depths but searched in vain
Ah! Tulasi
Yet sisters we cannot be

My prince I claimed. The curse vanquished.
In cut belly of fish, Fish-wit! The ring was found,
Proud I, adorned the vermillion dot.
Sparkled my pineal plane, beautiful.
But you? Bore the cross and lost your name.
For fourteen years grief in kingdom,
You were forever damned.
Forever "Hunchback".
Anger and pain, fright and spite, you.
Today you stand, puppet on strings,
Phenyl and pail along
Seek permission to enter, wordlessly scrub my floors.
So last command I give today, Go back!
Die there, from where you came!
And stubborn hold serene swan
But be fooled not! She is storm
Caress in reverence her downy feathers
Ved-anta they hold,
Hiding many books
O! Tulasi, hold any one
Only then can we
Sisters truly
Forever be.

Oulia! Rain Morn

Plops
Large single rain in my Tea
Best of first
Pat at Dawn
Boon showers soon lets drop
Tinsel film on blooms sedate
A sweep of bougainvillea, colourscape
Paper petals fine veined quiver
Try hold, shivers of tiny splash
Try hold, dance on dirt's decline

Whereas, rose-bud-like buds
Nestle, velveteen in cute warmth.
Startle at Her pitcher's pitter-patter
Then gulp dollops or lick a little
Snug-umm in snoozies, chleepy chweets
Dream of flower years, left awash, away!

While, Neem neebori full soaked ready
Falls bitter sweet as Neem tree made
Hue pale, trance-like in water scented mud
Among foliage, thorns and bark peels, say

Pure as sure call of hearts
Dulia!
Benediction of heaven,
You have come!

Yet the Feeler
Of one drop drunk
Long since has rolled
Warm flavor of
Tea best yet.

Eager waits

Beauty to Create
Together in Love
Eager waits!

Replete with sky
Pure Flower
Magnolia,
Queen
Rarest blue!

Replete with Ocean
Nectar filled
A Dewdrop
Sheathed fire
Particle proud!

With spoils of night
Forgotten, above
A drop sparkles,
Within tenuous petals.
Ocean's hint,
On rare tint of sky.
A Dewdrop
On Magnolia flower rests.

Etched perfectly,
On slate of night.
The pivot
Of countless,
Fulsome nights.

Crawls then,
Why?
Small, dark
Insect
Surreptitious
Inside?

En route Ahmedabad to Nabipur

Ate her, my window of A/C coach
Lost her, Nav Jeevan Express
Running away on slithering track
Lost her, sprawled
In known river's mad spate
Ballooned Frog in Monsoon broth

Mud spawns yet,
Hers will swim
Cry queasy long
Mudspawn cries.
Bunchhide in rottening plots
Of sticks and stones
Wriggle then
As a school of fish
In search of prey

Besiege on moonless night one day
Some Fateful day that!
Croak crack croak
Tail-less frogs
Devastate prey

She'll plea
And plea again,
"Come! Mad Spate
Deluge them away!"

No bridges were built
No linking done
She, in waters hysteria
I, on page.

Experimenting? Why so?

Mustering air, to
Forming clouds.
Confining particles,
Precipitating white
Markings in sky,
Dusting again...

Measuring moisture, to
Raising Mist.
Diffusing Sun,
Folding quiet liquids,
Vaporizing lakes.
Obliterating skies
Darkening ...

Ah! Those spirals,
Rising!
Mist for clouds
Enticing so!
Drawing lips,
Craving ...
Locking slowly
Touching...

And Parting
Freeing
Amidst Clouds
Amidst Mist
As Dove ...

Plunging!
Winging!
Dropping!
Flying!
Trying in experiments
Finding crystals!

Capsuled illuminations.
Illuminations jostling,
Shattering crystals,
Scattering shards.
Shards Sparkling!

Bits,
Forming Fractals,
Stringing,
Attaining,
Anew.

As Populace new
Ascribing
To You
Love, This is. This is loving.

Extraordinaire!
O! Hidden One
Experimenting?
Why so?

Eyes Open, Tortoise

Eyes open,
Tortoise
Wakes
In the face
And
Swims as
Whale.
Singing and
Swimming!
Flipping and
Whistling!
Racing and
Moving!
Stopping and
Watching...
Looking and
Wanting...
Coveting and
Seizing!
Gloating and
Eating!

Knowing, little yet,
Purple.
The prize,
A royal covet,
Encrusted in Time
And
Undefined Time
Anti or Pro matter
An elusive Core?
Is Baiting
And
Mutating...

Weed and Money Plant-Hanging

With mud, a wiry Plant throws
Twine sinewy to sap
Cream heart of Money plant
In Air!

Green plush, curls lush, Money Plant lurches,
Ornate with oils and gems of Bhaskara
For Mud!

Entwined,
Weed and Plant
Comb crinkled Croton kumkum rows.

Hot hands pluck
Plant from plant!
Mud from Air
Chandan from Oil
Twine from Curls
Wild from Tended

Chucked by Feeler!
At noonday high
Tendril and Twine
Sap and Heart

Insect and Shade
Smell and Spore
Quiet and Colours
Afternoon and Mellow!

Two hoots!
To Stupid
Impulse
At Core.

Oh! Feeler
You Preserve
Or Destroy?
Oh Feeler!
Gather your quest quickly
As Age mine
Has bronzed to Sun.

For Help

For help, reach out
With hands both
To the World
A Brush 'n paint
or
A Pail 'n brush,
They may
Them turn into.
Deem them then,
To
Some wall.
The wall,
Is for you
To choose.

Gate Tsunami

Fade Stars!
Moon rules
Marigold path
Stray!
Indicates

Night Queen
Flowers white
Moments perfume
Wisps
Inhale!

Sudden Bird
Shadow leaves
Brushes heights
Pangs!
Evoke

Such Delicates
Within
My Gates

Beyond,
I fear
Tormented waves
Tuneless tides
Tuneless...
Gate Tsunami!

Rain, God in Parts

God in parts!
Rains! Rain drops
How shall I hold
You
In my palm?

Full or Part
Saarang of my heart
How shall I hold
You
In my palm?

Brimful earthen pot
Resting in shade of parijat
Mukunda-sip sip!
Mynah's flutter flutter!
How shall I hold
You
In my palm?

Heavy Bakul, Gulmuhur
Liet motif durrie roll
Small Sunshine quick rests
Long black ants thread all!

How shall I hold
You
In my palm?

Glows First Star near Tree.
Quiet, sand grains sleep.
Rain parts, rivulets go on.
Calm collects a rippling song

How shall I hold
You
In my palm?

Saarang of my heart!
God in parts!

Me, Slowcoach

Me, Slowcoach.
Me, snail-pace
Call me a crab,
When no silver runs!

When on trail,
Beached Alone,
Shell.
Burrow in sand
And
Wait for tide.

On Way to Mamallapuram

Lucky dance to see!
Big waves of sea
On car glass, left
Dip tossed
Sun ball
Big Gold to right
Not-out!

Ode to Pale Moon

Stole you!
Pale Moon of dulled grace
Forgotten!
On flaked cloud pillows
Forlorn!
On grey sky-sheets

Hid you!
Waned one
From blatant stare of Arunodaya
As sashayed He
From parlours beyond,
In fashions of crimson,
Conjured tricks!
Drawing props
Of seven white steeds
Reined-in with better of gold.

Largesse, His Quickness dealt
On slumbers last quiet.

So
Glissades ruby
On Himavan peaks
To gush,
A few pearls, threw,

Into waters of Gangotri.
For jest,
Effulgence tippled
On dark leaf each.
Roved dreams
To eye lids weary,
To tattle of trees!
Then, confounded them all,
With impetuous blaze
From sudden heights.

Beg you, Pale Moon
Stay!
My whisper hear,
Held you child captive, near,
In cup 'o water, happy!
As mother cajoled, sang and fed
You did the child dance!

Silver-spun! Known you, long,
Gem ocean-rubble to moon-stone
And to the wearer's stone
Smile-in mystic twinkles
Of peace
Of love tones!

Felt you, Silver spate, splurge longings
On stone peaks, on still shores,
On still bodies, still at chores

Ignite the dormant, unlock them
All, Away to squander hours!

Found you, sliver sharp,
Goad green waters
Assemble frisky waves
Froth Lace in Race
To toss bubbles
On high shores.

Oh! Calm Apostle
Of fiery beauty atoned
Moistured eye, silvern gaze
In changeless face
Of forever God

Calming thrill
Of galactic gaze
For east, for west
On course, set

Darkness comes, yet
Oh! Lone travelling leveler
You Flow light
Light day!

A Feeler pleads
But, will you stay?

Rained Night... I Drink

Rained night
I drink
Single
Stark rose pink
Heightened on stalk
Petals in wine
Call of souls!
Light Swirls
Warm velvet
Swirl on...

Unseen Air movement
Heady subtleties, waft
Clasped in clasps
A Poem grows!
Skies Surrender
Scents yours
Squander!
Rose Is!

Must He
Now call?
I will not go.

Still Body
Drunk is
And
Spatial grows!
Drunk so!
Let be
More
Much more.

Rained night
I drink
Is Rose!
Is Rose!

Red Heaps Red

Red heaps Red
Memory petals
So vibrant, so strong
Maple memories
Chinar memories
Jasmine memories
Lie.
In Gulmuhur petals
Lava!
In mud trenches long.

Woman
With stick stokes
Picks pieces of petals
Still warm,
A heaven's sequel,
At no price.

Petals and She,
A haven for each other
Burn bright,
Wee wick,
Pierces
Twilight's calm.

Of bygone centuries,
From haven sometimes,
The spools, stories replay.
Our prince, Siddhartha
Saw those men.
With fibers live,
Don a ritual style,
To smash the mud,
Before the Star
Climbed high,
That five and five be one.

A final adieu
A bid, he knew
That five and five be one.
It was so then,
Still continues.

Scatter
Petal memories
Fire!
In blind gullies
Long.

So vibrant, so strong
Red heaps Red

Small Dangles Leaf Yellow

Small dangles leaf yellow
Broken web's end holding
In second sunshine
Gloats on
Caresses more all gleams
All longings.
In a whiff
The tug of last wave carries

Makes mound patches
On Earth,
Leaves yellow
Or free flows
On Ganga pure.
Around spring new
laughs and cries
Fast moving minute spider
Steel web spits

Matchless magic
In my mellowness, see
A Dew poised
On rainbow light
Bursts to quest
It's ephemerality

Tell us O Seer,
In silence complete.
How you grow?

So enthralling!
My leafy bough,
See how it grows!

Snake Unattended

Watch near
When far you look
A snake could be
At play.

Not always would he
The fence pole climb
Show his underbelly white
On weeded pathway.

Not always would
A Sunray stage,
A spotlight throw on him,
As Winds push leaves away.

Not always would
The gentle Mynah find
The wings to
Hover and chip,
Chip him away!
Or fluttering
Assemble
The Crow, the Koel and Parakeet
All
On Redressals Day

Summer Nights

Sun's beads, fingers beneath
Mango nights, fireflies enough!
Clammy laze,
In follicles core!
Stillnessness
Open door!

Unbraid, sweat crystals
Roll
Oh! Carelessness!
Cares to Sea shores!
At Sea and Shore
As sand, sand slip!
Shell, a
May smooth sole beneath.

Soul
Stand still!
Stand still!

Time pieces your World

Time pieces your World.
Watches and Clocks
Mine.
Timeless wound.
From feet to neck,
In yours rooted.
Head alone
Flowers
Grows
Dies
Grows...

Fireflies All! Lit bodies

Fireflies all! Lit bodies
Between Mango leaves,
Light and dim.
Hot air path craves,
In silences, erupts
Mesh of leaves,
Tearing.
Rolls on sand,
Slowly,
Sand
Defining.

Glossary

This glossary consists of explanations and/or meanings of words used in the poems. Some words are coined by the poet. These bring out a unique essence in the poem. The new coinages are italicized in this glossary.

Again

Anad (Sanskrit)-A vibration which cannot be felt/heard normally but can be by meditating on it, as believed by the ancient rishis/seers. It is the opposite of *naad*, meaning Sound in Sanskrit.

Aum (Sanskrit)-The sound/vibration believed to be synonymous with the Creator. It symbolizes the prana or life breath which runs through one's body.

Mynah-It is a bird that belongs to the *Starling family*. Mynahs are medium sized passerines with strong feet. Their flight is strong and direct. They are gregarious. Their plumage is typically dark brown. In India, the *Common Mynah* is found in plenty. These birds have a short yellow beak with eyes outlined in yellow as well. The scientific name for the common Mynah is *Acridotheres tristis.*

Tulsi-Ocimum Tenuifloram, or the Holy basil.

100 Meters or So

Bulbul-A beautiful little song bird. It has an amazing quality of constantly dancing while on ground! Bulbuls are a family, *Pycnonotidae* of medium sized, passerine, song birds. The family is distributed across most of Africa, Middle East, Tropical Asia, Indonesia, and also Japan. The word Bulbul is derived from Persian meaning nightingale, but in English Bulbuls refer to passerine birds of a different family.

Gulmuhur-Red, bright flowers, also known commonly as fire-flame flowers. The petals of this flower are spoon-shaped and spread out wide. The botanical name of Gulmuhur is *Delonix Regia.*

Jasmine-An evergreen semi-vining shrub. It grows to the height of 8-10 feet. The flower is about one inch. The flowers are white in colour. Its stems are slender, trailing, green and glaborous. The scientific name of Jasmine is *Jasminum.*

Must-Borrowed from Persian, and making its way into Urdu and Hindi, *Must* literally means drunk or inebriated. More accurately, it is used to mean a state of spiritual euphoria. It is used in various subtly or significantly different senses throughout Persian, Urdu and Hindi literature.

'Must' is a term which is also used when elephants are in heat.

Mynah-It is a bird that belongs to the *Starling family*. Mynahs are medium sized passerines with strong feet. Their flight is strong and direct. They are gregarious. Their plumage is typically dark brown. In India, the *Common Mynah* is found in plenty. These birds have a short yellow beak with eyes outlined in yellow as well. The scientific name for the common Mynah is *Acridotheres tristis*.

Aggression

Bakul-A tall majestic tree giving plenty of shade, and bearing tiny, white sweet smelling flowers.

Caesaaa-Exaggerated expression for emphasis of the word 'Caesar'.

Cattle trap-Typically, an iron grating in front of gates of bungalows, to prevent entry of stray cattle or goats, even if the gate is left open.

Cls-(exaggerated for emphasis to express mortifying control) Close.

Lab-(abbreviation) Labrador.

O Feeler-O Perceiver, receiver of messages from stimuli.

Ooopen-Exaggerated expression for emphasis of the word 'Open'.

Shepherd-German Shepherd.

Suprabhat-An Invocatory prayer in lyrical verses. Typically, these are sung early in the morning, in temples and homes.

Ur (Informal, abbreviation)-Your.

Body Feels Gold

Chandan-(Sanskrit) (noun) Sandal wood.

(adj) The colour of Sandalwood, or the oil extracted from the Sandal tree. The oil is highly valued for its fragrance.

Filigree-(noun) ornamental work of fine (typically gold or silver) wire formed into delicate tracery. This is a jewellery craft from Eastern India, Odisha.

Moon-kohl-Kohl or eye liner.

Sisters

Jamune-A large evergreen Asian tree of the myrtle family, which yields edible fruit which is dark purple in colour. The dried powdered kernel of the fruit is a home remedy for diabetes. The fruit is best avoided by singers before programmes! Could cause a bad throat.

Kutir (Sanskrit)-A spartan hut for ascetics in forests.

Mahua-An Indian Tropical tree, largely found in central and north India. *Madhuca longifolia* is the scientific name of this tree. It is cultivated in warm and humid regions for its oleaginous seeds (producing between 20 and 200 kg of seeds annually per tree, depending on maturity), flowers and wood. The fat (solid at ambient temperature) is used for the care of the skin, to manufacture soap or detergents, and as a vegetable butter. It can also be used as a fuel oil. The seed cakes obtained after extraction of oil constitute very good fertilizer. The dried fruits are used to produce an alcoholic drink in tropical India.

Naad-The basic sound for music.

Raaga-A set of notes in Indian classical music ranging usually from 5 to 9, in which songs are based.

Ved-anta (Sanskrit)-The end of Knowledge. The four Vedas, Rig, Yajur Sama Atharva are the four Vedas which consist comprehensive study of different fields of knowledge.

Bakul-Bakul is an evergreen tree found in the tropical forests in South Asia, South East Asia and Northern Australia. It is called Bakul in Sanskrit. When in bloom the Bakul produces sweet smelling, tiny flowers. These flowers are also considered sacred among the many exotic, flowering trees, in India.

Dulia Rain Morn'

Chleepy-(baby-talk or child/pet-directed speech for) Sleepy.

Chweets (Pl.)-(baby-talk or child/pet-directed speech for) Sweet.

Dulia-(Greek) Reverence accorded to saints and angels.

Neem nibori-(Hindi)-Seed of the Neem tree, very common on the Indian landscape and valued for the medicinal properties of its leaves and seeds.

Snoozies (Pl.) Snoozes.

Snug-umm-(adj) (baby-talk or child/pet-directed speech for) snug and cozy.

God in Parts

Bakul-A tall majestic tree giving plenty of shade, and bearing tiny, white sweet smelling flowers.

Durrie-a thick rug woven with colorful designs.

Gulmuhur-Red, bright flowers, also known commonly as fire-flame flowers. The petals of this flower are spoon-shaped and spread out wide. They are used in some medicenes. The Gulmuhur trees are used as avenue trees. The botanical name of Gulmuhur is *Delonix Regia.*

Mukunda-One of the numerous names of Lord Krishna.

Parijat-a sweet smelling, small and very tender white flower with an orange stalk.

Saarang-A group of musical notes that creates a melody/*raga.*

To Kill a Poet

Forgivenessness (noun)-The nature that underlies the thought, attitude and action of forgiving.

Juhi (Hindi)-Jasmine flower.

Junta-Anglicized form of Janata, meaning, people.

Spreadnessness (noun)-The nature and vastness of that which spreads.

Pale Moon

Arunodaya (Sanskrit)-Sunrise.

Himavan-(Indian Mythology) King of mountains, embodiment of the Himalayan mountains.

Gangotri-The origin of the Ganga in the Himalayas.

Red Heaps Red

Chinar-A tall, deciduous tree found largely in Kashmir, known for its clover shaped leaves which turn deep red in autumn.

Five and Five be one: A reference to Indian philosophy (pancha-bhuta) that the five elements which make up the world are essentially the same as the five elements that make up the body.

Gullies-(Hindi) narrow lanes in towns.

Gulmuhur-Red, bright flowers, also known commonly as fire-flame flowers. The petals of this flower are spoon-shaped and spread out wide. The botanical name of Gulmuhur is *Delonix Regia.*

Siddhartha-Siddhartha Gautama (full name) also known as Buddha, the 'enlightened one'. He taught "Ahimsa" or non-violence was the only path to happiness for mankind.

Weed and Money Plant

Bhaskara (Sanskrit)-One of the many names of the Sun.

Chandan (Hindi)-Sandal wood.

Kumkum-(Sanskrit) It is a red colored powder used as an adornment on the forehead. It is made from turmeric or any other local material.

When turmeric is dried and powdered with a bit of slaked lime it turns into a deep red.

Will Some Body with Me Not Dally

Chandrima (Sanskrit)-The Moon.

Neem (Hindi)-Margosa.

Buffalo Stroll

Ugh (slang)-Filth.

Dhaivata The sixth note in the D major scale of Indian Music.

Small dangles leaf yellow

Ganga-One of the names of the Ganges river.

Snake Unattended

Mynah-It is a bird that belongs to the *Starling family*. Mynahs are medium sized passerines with strong feet. Their flight is strong and direct. They are gregarious. Their plumage is typically dark brown. In India, the *Common Mynah* is found in plenty. These birds have a short yellow beak with eyes outlined in yellow as well. The scientific name for the common Mynah is *Acridotheres tristis.*

Summer Nights

Stillnessness-(noun) the nature of quietitude.